THE QUICK AND HEALTHY BLENDER RECIPE COOKBOOK

MARIANNE B HUFFMAN

Copyright © 2023 Marianne B Huffman

All rights reserved.

INTRODUCTION

In today's fast-paced world, maintaining a healthy and balanced lifestyle can be quite a challenge. With so many responsibilities and commitments, it's often difficult to find the time to prepare nutritious meals and snacks. The good news is that you don't have to compromise on health or taste to enjoy satisfying and delicious food. Introducing "The Easy Blender Recipe Book," your go-to guide for creating delectable, nutrient-packed smoothies that cater to your specific health and wellness needs.

Smoothies are not only a convenient way to enjoy a variety of fruits, vegetables, and other nutrient-dense ingredients but also a delightful way to nourish your body from the inside out. With the help of this book, you'll learn how to make delicious and nourishing smoothies that cater to a range of goals: improving heart health, promoting detoxification, supporting weight loss, enhancing skin radiance, boosting energy, promoting anti-aging, and incorporating superfoods.

Chapter 1 sets the stage by discussing the numerous health benefits of smoothies. You'll learn about the vital nutrients, antioxidants, and vitamins that can be found in smoothies, helping you understand why they're so beneficial for your overall well-being. This chapter will also touch on the importance of consuming a diverse array of fruits and vegetables for optimal health.

In Chapter 2, we'll delve into the process of making smoothies with the Nutribullet, a popular and powerful blender designed specifically for creating smooth and creamy smoothie concoctions. This section will cover essential tips and tricks to ensure that your smoothies come out perfect every time, as well as provide guidance on selecting the best ingredients and combining them for maximum nutritional benefit.

From Chapters 3 to 9, you'll discover a wealth of smoothie recipes that cater to different health objectives. Each chapter focuses on a specific goal and features ten tantalizing smoothie recipes that not only taste great but also provide your body with the nutrients it needs to thrive.

Chapter 3, for example, focuses on heart health, offering smoothie recipes that are packed with ingredients known to support cardiovascular well-being. Chapters 4 and 5 feature detoxification and weight loss smoothies, respectively, with an emphasis on ingredients that aid in cleansing the body and promoting a healthy metabolism.

In Chapter 6, you'll find smoothie recipes for radiant skin, with a focus on ingredients that nourish the skin and promote a glowing complexion. Chapter 7 is all about energy-boosting smoothies, while Chapter 8 highlights anti-aging concoctions to help you look and feel youthful for years to come.

Chapter 9 is devoted to superfood smoothies, showcasing recipes that incorporate some of the most nutrient-dense ingredients on the planet. These smoothies are not only delicious but also loaded with vitamins, minerals, antioxidants, and other health-promoting compounds.

Finally, in Chapter 10, we'll discuss how to reap the benefits of fulfilling smoothies in your everyday life. This chapter will provide tips on incorporating smoothies into your daily routine and maximizing their nutritional value to support a healthy and vibrant lifestyle.

"The Easy Blender Recipe Book" is designed to inspire and empower you to take control of your health and well-being through the simple and enjoyable act of blending smoothies. With 60 delectable recipes and a wealth of information about the benefits of smoothie consumption, you'll be well-equipped to harness the power of your blender and create tasty, health-promoting beverages in the comfort of your own home.

No matter your health goals or dietary preferences, this book has something for everyone. So go ahead, dust off your blender, and get ready to embark on a journey towards better health, one satisfying smoothie at a time.

As you progress through "The Easy Blender Recipe

Book," you will come to appreciate the versatility of smoothies and the ease with which you can customize them to suit your taste buds and nutritional needs. Whether you're a seasoned smoothie aficionado or a curious novice, this book will serve as a valuable resource, providing you with the tools and inspiration needed to create healthful, delicious concoctions.

One of the key advantages of smoothies is their convenience. In today's world, time is often scarce, and many people struggle to find the hours needed to prepare wholesome meals. Smoothies are a fantastic solution to this problem, as they can be made in minutes and consumed on the go. By incorporating smoothies into your daily routine, you'll be able to nourish your body with essential nutrients while maintaining your busy lifestyle.

Another compelling aspect of smoothies is their ability to accommodate a wide variety of dietary needs and preferences. Whether you follow a vegan, gluten-free, paleo, or low-carb diet, smoothies can be tailored to meet your specific requirements. This book includes a diverse array of recipes that cater to different dietary lifestyles, ensuring that everyone can enjoy the benefits of nutrient-dense smoothies.

Furthermore, smoothies can play a significant role in promoting sustainable, eco-friendly eating habits. By using seasonal, locally-sourced produce in your smoothie creations, you'll be supporting local farmers and reducing your carbon footprint. Additionally, smoothies are an excellent way to utilize overripe fruits and vegetables, minimizing food waste and promoting a more sustainable approach to nutrition.

As you begin to explore the world of smoothies, you may find yourself inspired to experiment with new ingredients and flavor combinations. "The Easy Blender Recipe Book" encourages creativity and innovation in the kitchen, providing you with the knowledge and confidence needed to craft your own unique smoothie recipes. Feel free to play around with different fruits, vegetables, nuts, seeds, and liquids to create smoothies that are tailored to your preferences and nutritional needs.

In addition to the 60 mouthwatering smoothie recipes featured in this book, you'll also find valuable tips on storing and freezing ingredients, as well as guidance on selecting the best produce for optimal flavor and nutritional content. These practical tips will help you streamline your smoothie-making process, making it even easier to incorporate these nourishing beverages into your daily routine.

Whether you're looking to improve your overall health, support specific wellness goals, or simply enjoy a delicious and refreshing beverage, "The Easy Blender Recipe Book" is your ultimate guide to unlocking the full potential of your blender. With this comprehensive resource in hand, you'll be well on your way to enjoying a healthier, more vibrant lifestyle, one delightful smoothie at a time.

So, let's embark on this exciting culinary adventure together, blending our way to better health and well-being. Cheers to a happier, healthier you!

CONTENTS

Chapter 1 – Health Benefits of Smoothies 1

Chapter 2 – Making Smoothies with Nutribullet – The Process 3

Chapter 3 – 10 Smoothie Recipes for a Healthy Heart 6

Blueberry and Avocado Smoothie 7

Chia Seed Rainforest Smoothie 8

Berry Heart Healthy Smoothie 9

Green Lemonade Smoothie... 10

Healthy Heart Smoothie... 11

Orange and Berry Smoothie 12

Berry Pomegranate Smoothie 13

Heart Improvement Smoothie.. 14

Healthy Heart Acai, Avocado Smoothie.......................... 15

Smart Heart Smoothie 16

Chapter 4 – 10 Smoothie Recipes for Detoxification 17

Berry Breakfast Smoothie 18

Super Green Smoothie 19

Veggie Smoothie 20

Sweet Spirit Smoothie 21

Blissfully Tasty Smoothie 22

Belly Soothing Smoothie 23

Yummy Green Smoothie 24

Strawberry Fields Smoothie 25

Sicilian Smoothie 26

Lemon Blueberry Smoothie 27

Chapter 5 – 10 Smoothie Recipes for Weight Loss ... 28

Green Slimming Smoothie 29

Banana Peanut Butter Smoothie 30

Sweet Spinach Smoothie 31

Morning Smoothie 32

Vegan Vanilla Smoothie 33

Flat Belly Smoothie 34

Vitamin C Smoothie 35

Apple and Cinnamon Smoothie 36

Chia Berry Smoothie.. 37

Vitamin Smoothie... 38

Chapter 6 – 10 Smoothie Recipes for Radiant Skin .. 39

Smoothie for Glowing Skin 40

Pretty Pear Smoothie.. 41

Berry Medley Smoothie 42

Green beauty Smoothie 43

Smoothie for Radiant Skin 44

Wrinkle Fighting Smoothie 45

Almond Flax Smoothie 46

Green Beautifier Smoothie 47

Beautifying Smoothie 48

Almond Milk Smoothie 49

Chapter 7 – 10 Smoothie Recipes for Energy Boost. 50

Killer Kale Smoothie 51

Silky Blueberry and Chia Smoothie 52

Shamrock Smoothie 53

Beetroot and Apple Smoothie 54

Apple Pie Smoothie 55

Spinach Peanut Butter Smoothie 56

Cantaloupe and Lemon Smoothie 57

Sharon Fruit and Blackberry Smoothie 58

Dark Chocolate and Spinach Smoothie 59

Blueberry Smoothie 60

Chapter 8 – 10 Smoothie Recipes for Anti- Aging 61

Antioxidant Anti-Aging Smoothie 62

Beauty Bonanza Smoothie 63

Green Smoothie for Anti-Aging 64

Coconut Bliss Smoothie 65

Berry Smoothie 66

Delectable Goodness 67

Chia and Blueberry Smoothie 68

Soy Milk Smoothie 69

Celery and Spinach Smoothie 70

Dewy Skin Smoothie 71

Chapter 9 – 10 Smoothie Recipes for Super Foods .. 72

Blueberry and Cocoa Smoothie 73

Mint Chip Smoothie 74

Pineapple and Kale Smoothie 75

Raw Mint Chocolate Smoothie 76

Super Smoothie 77

Protein Smoothie 78

Aloe Vera Lemonade Smoothie 79

Bananarama Smoothie Recipe 80

T-Mac Smoothie 81

Cilantro Smoothie 82

Chapter 10 – Reaping the Benefits from Fulfilling Smoothies 83

Chapter 1 – Health Benefits of Smoothies

Smoothies are one of the quickest and easiest ways of nourishing your body with the required nutrients. Make the smoothies yourself, and adjust the ingredients according to your taste, it is that simple. All you need is the Nutribullet blender and voila, in just a matter of seconds, you have a satisfying breakfast or snack.

Most people wonder why they should have smoothies in the first place. Well that's because when you want an all in one package; smoothies are your best bet. This chapter will give you information regarding the various benefits you stand to gain by having smoothies daily. After reading all the benefits you stand to gain by consuming smoothies every day, you will immediately want to start making and enjoying them.

Fruit and vegetable smoothies have many health benefits. These benefits are listed out below. Go through them and be amazed with how just a glass of smoothie can provide you everything you need to spend a healthy and happy life.

- Smoothies offer a pure source of nutrition, as they are free from any preservatives or chemicals, and are entirely natural, especially when made fresh.
- The amount of nutrients you receive from a glass of smoothie is dependent upon the types and quantity of fruits and vegetables you have used in it. Since most fruits and vegetables are rich in Vitamins A and C, potassium, magnesium, and other such minerals and Vitamins, you can be sure to receive a good amount of nutrition from them.
- Smoothies are much better than juices, whether of fruits or vegetables, for they also contain fiber, which juices lack. Apart

- from that, they are also quite filling, as you make use of whole fruits and vegetables.
- When you combine fruits and vegetables together in order to make smoothies, you can make use of all those vegetables that you usually avoid. The taste is so delicious, that you end up consuming them without even noticing that you are having veggies you secretly dislike.
- Most people do not consume vegetables on a daily basis, making them deficient in some of the nutrients that are essential for the body. With smoothies, you can even out your body's requirements, as the taste is masked by the fruity flavor.
- One of the best things about smoothies is that they can be prepared very quickly. All you need are the ingredients, assembled in one place, and a blender, the pulse and voila, your smoothie is prepared.
- Smoothies provide you with lasting source of energy that helps you in staying alert and fit for the whole day. What more could you want?
- They are also a great way to remain fit, and shed those extra pounds as you are having nutrient dense meals with out those extra calories.

A great weight loss method, source of nutrition, energy and healthy fibers, essential for your body, smoothies are a great way to start your day. Are you ready to start blending and making smoothies that are lip smacking good?

Chapter 2 – Making Smoothies with Nutribullet – The Process

When you want to create highly nutritious smoothies, then Nutribullet is one if the best tools to use. It is exceptionally easy to use. Crushing fruits and converting them into pulp has never been easier. It even has the ability to extract nutrients from seeds and stems of fruits and vegetables, thereby ensuring that you get the maximum amount of nutrition for your body.

Nuts, vegetables, and any other kind of food can be turned into creamy, delicious, lip smacking goodness. You can enjoy protein shakes, and smoothies at any time of the day. Your job is made easier and you can easily make smoothies using any ingredient. Every time you feel like enjoying the pop of flavors in your mouth, Nutribullet will make the job easier.

When using the Nutribullet, you can be sure to obtain a smoothie that is smooth and velvety in texture. This blender does not leave any chunks, unless you want it to. Nutribullet has a high powered motor, which when combined with its patented blade design, along with its ultra-fast cyclonic actions, allows it to extract all the essential nutrients. This gives your smoothies, a little extra energy boost.

And, the best part of all, it includes all the fiber, that the fruits and vegetables have to offer. It breaks down the fibers and liquefies them, an ability which is not present in any blender. This device is a two in one combination of a juicer and a blender, thereby, providing you with the final product that is simply divine in its taste.

All you have to do is place the fruits and vegetables in the Nutribullet, flip the switch on and let the Nutribullet do its magic of transforming the vegetable and fruit into a smooth liquid. In just 30 seconds, you will have the perfectly liquefied smoothie. Enjoy it on your own, with your friends and family or have it on the go.

Make sure to wash and dice the fruits and vegetables you are using, place the vegetable first and then the fruits. Fill half the tall or small cup with the vegetable and then add the fruit pieces. Top up with water or any other fluid you are using and then screw on the lid, which has the extractor blades attached. Whizz it up, and voila, you have creamy and yummy smoothies right there with you. Only whizz it for 35-40 seconds. Do not go over one minute, to avoid straining the motor; and you might end up with a repair on your hands.

In only 30-40 seconds your delicious smoothie is prepared, what more could you ask for? Oh and one more thing, no need to waste time transferring the smoothie to a glass or cup, you can drink it straight from the Nutribullet cup. It even has a lid, which fits right on, making it easier to carry it around with you to work. Impressive, don't you think?

Before we move on to the smoothies, I would like to repeat the instructions of the order of placing the ingredients in the Nutribullet cup. **You must put the ingredients in the following order.**

1) First, fill half the tall or short cup with the green leafy vegetables and then place the chopped fruits on top.

2) Then add in the dry ingredients like nuts, seeds, or protein powder (if you are using these ingredients).

3) Top up with liquid such as water, almond milk or coconut milk or coconut water.

And let the Nutribullet work its magic. Only ice shavings should be blended. Smoothies can be served with ice cubes if required.

All right, now that you have learned all of the essential details, let us get right down to the focus of this book, which are smooth and delectable smoothies.

Chapter 3 – 10 Smoothie Recipes for a Healthy Heart

Having a healthy heart will help you in staying in shape. Increasing your fiber intake will help you in keeping your arteries strong and healthy. You also need to watch your cholesterol, so, cut down on those fries and burgers you have every day. Having smoothies instead of junk food, will help you in remaining fit and smart, not to mention attractive.

Here are 10 smoothies for your healthy heart. Have these every day, and feel the difference yourself.

Blueberry and Avocado Smoothie

Ingredients

- 1/4 cup frozen blueberries
- 1/4 cup avocado
- The juice of 1/2 a lime
- A handful of Kale leaves
- 1 tbsp of vanilla whey protein powder, or any other non-dairy protein powder
- 1 tsp of raw, pure honey
- 4 ice cubes, shavings
- Top up to the line with coconut water

Directions

Fill half of the cup with the kale. Add the other ingredients. Top up to the line on the cup with coconut water. Use only ice shavings if blending the ice.

Nutritional Information

- Calories 268
- Saturated Fat 7.9g
- Carbohydrate 47g
- Sodium 54mg
- Fiber 7g

Chia Seed Rainforest Smoothie

Ingredients

- 1 cup spinach
- 1 cup acai berries, fresh or dried
- 1 tbsp chia seeds
- 2 broccoli florets
- Stevia, to taste
- Top up with 1/2 - 1 cup unsweetened almond milk

Directions

Fill half of the Nutribullet cup with the spinach. Add the rest of the ingredients. Top up with almond milk. Blend until smooth and serve.

Nutritional Information

- Calories 173
- Saturated Fat 2.2g
- Carbohydrate 13g
- Sodium 221mg
- Fiber 8g

Berry Heart Healthy Smoothie

Ingredients

- 1 tbsp hemp protein powder
- A handful of spinach leaves
- A handful of Kale leaves
- 1/2 cup blueberries
- 1/2 banana
- Top up with 1/2 - 1 cup almond milk

Directions

Fill the Nutribullet cup with spinach and kale leaves. Add the rest of the ingredients and blend until smooth. Enjoy while keeping your heart healthy.

Nutritional Information

- Calories 237
- Saturated Fat 0.6g
- Carbohydrate 38g
- Sodium 235mg
- Fiber 10g

Green Lemonade Smoothie

Ingredients

- 1 green apple chopped
- 1 cup Kale leaves
- 1 lemon juice and the zest, organic
- Top up with chilled water
- 3-4 ice cubes

Directions

Fill the cup with kale leaves first followed by the other ingredients except the ice cubes. Blend thoroughly and serve, garnished with a slice of lemon and the ice cubes. Enjoy this refreshing smoothie especially on a hot day.

Nutritional Information

- Calories 129
- Saturated Fat 0.1g
- Carbohydrate 33g
- Sodium 51mg
- Fiber 7g

Healthy Heart Smoothie

Ingredients

- A handful of spinach leaves
- 1/2 cup frozen raspberries
- 1 tsp dark cocoa powder
- 1/2 ripe banana
- Top up 1/2 - 1 cup semi-skimmed milk
- 3 ice cubes to be added to the smoothie

Directions

Fill half of the Nutribullet cup with the spinach leaves. Add all the rest of the solid ingredients. Top up with the semi-skimmed milk. Blend thoroughly. Serve with the ice cubes and enjoy.

Nutritional Information

- Calories 236
- Saturated Fat 3.3g
- Carbohydrate 40g
- Sodium 141mg
- Fiber 4g

Orange and Berry Smoothie

Ingredients

- 1/4 cup blueberries
- 1/4 cup chopped carrots
- 1/4 cup bananas
- A handful of kale leaves
- Squeeze of half a lemon
- 1/4 cup orange segments

Directions

Fill half the cup with the kale leaves followed by the rest of the ingredients. Top up with water to the line on the cup. Blend well. Serve, garnish with a slice of lemon and enjoy.

Nutritional Information

- Calories 146
- Saturated Fat 0.2g
- Carbohydrate 35g
- Sodium 58mg
- Fiber 7g

Berry Pomegranate Smoothie

Ingredients

- 1/2 cup of spinach leaves
- 1/4 cup blueberries, frozen or fresh
- 1/4 cup pomegranate
- 1/4 cup carrot, chopped
- 1/4 cup cucumber, chopped
- 1/2 tsp lemon zest
- 1/2 tsp fresh lemon juice
- 3-5 ice cubes

Directions

Place all the ingredients except the ice cubes in the Nutribullet blender, top up with water and then pulse until smooth. Remove the lid and then add in the ice cubes, and enjoy.

Nutritional Information

- Calories 78
- Saturated Fat 0.1g
- Carbohydrate 18g
- Sodium 37mg
- Fiber 4g

Heart Improvement Smoothie

Ingredients

- 1/4 cup pomegranate juice
- 1/4 cup cucumber, chopped
- 1/4 cup strawberries, fresh or frozen
- 1/2 banana
- A handful of Kale leaves
- 1/2 cup yogurt
- Top up with water

Directions

Fill the cup with kale leaves. Add the rest of the ingredients. Top up with water to the line. Blend, serve and enjoy this delicious smoothie, which helps in improving the blood circulation in your body, by making your heart stronger.

Nutritional Information

- Calories 223
- Saturated Fat 2.6g
- Carbohydrate 41g
- Sodium 95mg
- Fiber 5g

Healthy Heart Acai, Avocado Smoothie

Ingredients

- 1/2 cup of Swiss chard
- 1/2 cup acai berries, frozen
- 1 tbsp flaxseeds
- 1/2 avocado
- Fill to the line with coconut water

Directions

Fill half the cup with the Swiss chard. Add the rest of the ingredients. Top up with water to the line. Blend, serve and enjoy

Nutritional Information

- Calories 250
- Saturated Fat 3g
- Carbohydrate 19g
- Sodium 171mg
- Fiber 11g

Smart Heart Smoothie

Ingredients

- 1/2 tbsp flaxseed oil
- 1/2 cup cucumber, chopped
- 1/2 small banana, ripe
- Handful of Kale leaves and spinach
- 1/4 cup blueberries, fresh or frozen
- Top with water

Directions

Fill half of the cup with the kale and spinach leaves. Add the rest of the ingredients. Top up with water. Blend thoroughly and enjoy.

Nutritional Information

- Calories 165
- Saturated Fat 0.7g
- Carbohydrate 26g
- Sodium 32mg
- Fiber 5g

Chapter 4 – 10 Smoothie Recipes for Detoxification

Detoxification is very important for the body, for it helps in getting rid of all the toxins that might negatively affect the body. Enjoy while detoxifying with these recipes.

Berry Breakfast Smoothie

Ingredients

- 1/2 cup of leave of your choice
- 1/4 cup cherries, fresh
- 1/4 cup raspberries, frozen or fresh
- 1/4 cup carrots, chopped
- 1/4 tbsp ginger, freshly grated
- 1/4 cup cucumber, chopped
- 1 tsp flaxseed, ground
- 1 tbsp honey, raw and pure
- 2 tsp lemon juice
- Top up with 1/2 - 1 cup unsweetened almond milk, chilled

Directions

Fill half of the cup with lettuce. Add the rest of the ingredients. Blend and enjoy.

Nutritional Information

- Calories 195
- Saturated Fat 0.5g
- Carbohydrate 39g
- Sodium 222mg
- Fiber 7g

Super Green Smoothie

Ingredients

- 1 cup Kale leaves, chopped
- 1 medium celery rib, chopped
- 1/2 green apple
- 1/2 avocado
- 1/4 cup mint
- 1/4 tsp Green tea powder
- Top up with water

Directions

Fill half of the cup with the kale leaves. Add the rest of the ingredients. Top up with water to the line on the cup.

Nutritional Information

- Calories 220
- Saturated Fat 1.8g
- Carbohydrate 28g
- Sodium 88mg
- Fiber 12g

Veggie Smoothie

Ingredients

- 1/2 pear
- 3 slices cucumber
- 1/2 lemon (juice of)
- 1 scoop of protein powder
- 1/4 avocado
- A handful Kale, chopped
- A handful of cilantro leaves
- 2 tbsp ginger, fresh
- Top up with 1/2 - 1 cup coconut water

Directions

Fill half of the cup with kale. Add the rest of the ingredients. Top up with the coconut water. Blend until smooth, serve and enjoy.

Nutritional Information

- Calories 258
- Saturated Fat 1.5g
- Carbohydrate 35g
- Sodium 123mg
- Fiber 10g

Sweet Spirit Smoothie

Ingredients

- 1/2 banana
- 1/4 avocado
- A handful of Kale leaves
- 1/4 cup almond milk
- 1/4 cup blueberries
- 1 scoop of vanilla protein powder
- Water, as required

Directions

Fill half of the cup with the kale leaves. Add the rest of the ingredients. Top up to the line with water. Blend until smooth, serve in a glass and enjoy.

Nutritional Information

- Calories 194
- Saturated Fat 1.1g
- Carbohydrate 31g
- Sodium 132mg
- Fiber 8g

Blissfully Tasty Smoothie

Ingredients

- 1/2 pear
- 1 cup spinach leaves, chopped
- 1/4 cup coconut water
- 1/4 cup avocado, diced
- 1/2 cup carrots, chopped
- 1 cup almond milk
- 1 tsp chia seeds
- 1 apple

Directions

Fill half of the cup with spinach leaves. Add the rest of the ingredients. Top up with the almond milk. Blend thoroughly, serve and enjoy.

Nutritional Information

- Calories 285
- Saturated Fat 1.4g
- Carbohydrate 51g
- Sodium 316mg
- Fiber 14g

Belly Soothing Smoothie

Ingredients

- 1 cup papaya
- 1 cup of romaine lettuce
- 1/4 cucumbers
- The juice of 1/2 a lime
- 1 tbsp honey, raw and natural
- 1 cup coconut milk

Directions

Fill half of the cup with romaine lettuce. Add the rest of the ingredients. Top up with the coconut milk. Blend thoroughly, serve and enjoy.

Nutritional Information

- Calories 687
- Saturated Fat 49.8g
- Carbohydrate 51g
- Sodium 56mg
- Fiber 9g

Yummy Green Smoothie

Ingredients

- 1/4 large cucumber, chopped
- 1 cup Kale leaves, chopped
- 3 broccoli florets
- 1 orange, peeled, and segmented
- 1/2 green apple, chopped
- 1 cup romaine lettuce, chopped
- 1/2 lemon, peeled, and diced
- Top up with water

Directions

Fill half of the cup with the kale leaves. Add the rest of the ingredients. Top up to the line with water. Blend thoroughly, serve with 2-3 mint leaves (optional) and enjoy.

Nutritional Information

- Calories 182
- Saturated Fat 0.2g
- Carbohydrate 43g
- Sodium 50mg
- Fiber 11g

Strawberry Fields Smoothie

Ingredients

- 1/4 cup cashew nuts
- 1 tbsp lemon zest
- 1 small orange's segments
- 1/2 banana
- 1/4 cucumber, chopped
- 2 cups fresh strawberries
- 1 cup spinach leaves

Directions

Fill half of the cup with spinach leaves. Add the rest of the ingredients. Top up with water. Blend, serve and enjoy.

Nutritional Information

- Calories 384
- Saturated Fat 3.3g
- Carbohydrate 57g
- Sodium 36mg
- Fiber 11g

Sicilian Smoothie

Ingredients

- 1/4 cup carrots, chopped
- 1 cup spinach, chopped
- 1/4 red bell pepper, cubed
- 1/2 apple, cored, and chopped
- 1/4 large tomato, diced
- 1/4 celery stalk, chopped
- 1/4 cup watercress
- Top up with water

Directions

Fill half of the cup with the spinach. Add the rest of the ingredients. Top up with water. Blend and serve.

Nutritional Information

- Calories 84
- Saturated Fat 0.1g
- Carbohydrate 19g
- Sodium 65mg
- Fiber 5g

Lemon Blueberry Smoothie

Ingredients

- 1 cup water
- 1 cup blueberries, fresh
- A handful of spinach leaves
- 1 lemon, whole, chopped

Directions

Fill half of the cup with spinach. Add the rest of the ingredients. Top up to the line with water. Blend thoroughly.

Nutritional Information

- Calories 100
- Saturated Fat 0.1g
- Carbohydrate 26g
- Sodium 31mg
- Fiber 5g

Chapter 5 – 10 Smoothie Recipes for Weight Loss

If you want to shed, those extra few pound you've gained over the years and slim down to be even fitter and healthier, then, having these smoothies are a great way to go about it. Losing weight has never been easier; all you have to do is follow the recipes provided below.

Green Slimming Smoothie

Ingredients

- 1 cup spinach
- 1/4 bunch of parsley
- 1/4 cucumber, diced
- A bunch of mint
- 1/2 apple
- 1/4 lime
- 1/4 lemon
- Top up with water

Directions

Fill half of the cup with spinach. Add the rest of the ingredients. Top up with water. Blend thoroughly, serve and enjoy this slimming drink.

Nutritional Information

- Calories 81
- Saturated Fat 0.2g
- Carbohydrate 20g
- Sodium 41mg
- Fiber 6g

Banana Peanut Butter Smoothie

Ingredients

- 1/2 cup iceberg lettuce
- 1/2 cup coconut milk
- 1/2 banana
- 1 tbsp chocolate whey protein powder
- 1/2 cup crunchy peanut butter
- 6 ice cubes

Directions

Fill half of the cup with iceberg lettuce. Add the rest of the ingredients. Top up with coconut milk. Blend thoroughly. Serve and enjoy this filling and energizing drink.

Nutritional Information

- Calories 475
- Saturated Fat 26.5g
- Carbohydrate 26g
- Sodium 173mg
- Fiber 6g

Sweet Spinach Smoothie

Ingredients

- 1 cup spinach
- 7 green grapes
- a few pieces of pear
- 2 tbsp lime juice
- 1/4 cup cucumber, chopped
- Top with almond milk
- Frozen grapes for garnish

Directions

Fill half of the cup with spinach. Add the rest of the ingredients. Top up with almond milk. Blend thoroughly. Serve with the frozen grapes. Enjoy!

Nutritional Information

- Calories 129
- Saturated Fat 0.4g
- Carbohydrate 25g
- Sodium 211mg
- Fiber 5g

Morning Smoothie

Ingredients

- 2 oz Vanilla Greek Yogurt, fat free
- 1/2 cup Swiss chard
- 1 cup frozen strawberries
- 5 almonds
- 1/2 apple, cored and chopped
- 3/4 cup green tea
- 1/4 tsp cinnamon

Directions

Fill half of the cup with the Swiss chard. Add the rest of the ingredients. Top up to the line with water. Blend thoroughly and serve.

Nutritional Information

- Calories 194
- Saturated Fat 0.3g
- Carbohydrate 33g
- Sodium 192mg
- Fiber 8g

Vegan Vanilla Smoothie

Ingredients

- 1/2 cup soft tofu
- 1/2 banana, frozen, and chopped
- A handful of spinach leaves
- 1/2 cup vanilla soy milk
- 1/2 tbsp peanut butter

Directions

Fill half of the cup with the spinach leaves. Add the rest of the ingredients. Top up with water. Blend until smooth and serve. Makes a good lunch.

Nutritional Information

- Calories 211
- Saturated Fat 1.2g
- Carbohydrate 24g
- Sodium 103mg
- Fiber 4g

Flat Belly Smoothie

Ingredients

- 3 oz Vanilla Greek Yogurt, non fat
- 1/2 cup blueberries, frozen or fresh
- 2-3 florets of broccoli and/or cauliflower
- 1 tbsp almond butter
- 1/2 cup Romaine lettuce
- Top with water

Directions

Fill half of the cup with the Romaine lettuce. Add the rest of the ingredients. Top up to the line with water. Blend thoroughly. Serve and enjoy.

Nutritional Information

- Calories 199
- Saturated Fat 0.7g
- Carbohydrate 19g
- Sodium 48mg
- Fiber 4g

Vitamin C Smoothie

Ingredients

- 1 cup strawberries
- 1/4 cucumber
- 1/2 orange, peeled and segmented
- 3 Ice cube shavings
- A handful of Kale leaves
- 1 slice cantaloupe
- 1/4 tomato

Directions

Fill half of the cup with the kale leaves. Add all of the other ingredients. Blend thoroughly until smooth, serve in a glass and enjoy.

Nutritional Information

- Calories 189
- Saturated Fat 0.2g
- Carbohydrate 44g
- Sodium 60mg
- Fiber 10g

Apple and Cinnamon Smoothie

Ingredients

- 5 almonds, raw
- A handful of spinach leaves
- 1 red apple, cored, and diced
- 1/2 cup non fat milk
- 1/4 tsp cinnamon
- Top with coconut water

Directions

Fill half of the cup with spinach. Add the rest of the ingredients. Top up with coconut water. Blend thoroughly. Serve and enjoy.

Nutritional Information

- Calories 200
- Saturated Fat 0.6g
- Carbohydrate 35g
- Sodium 203mg
- Fiber 7g

Chia Berry Smoothie

Ingredients

- 1/2 cup pomegranate juice, unsweetened
- 1 cup of frozen berries, a mixture of raspberry, blueberry, blackberry, strawberry,
- A handful of romaine lettuce
- 1/2 tbsp chia seeds
- Top with water

Directions

Fill half of the cup with the Romaine lettuce. Add the rest of the ingredients. Top up to the line with water. Blend and serve.

Nutritional Information

- Calories 162
- Saturated Fat 0.2g
- Carbohydrate 39g
- Sodium 23mg
- Fiber 5g

Vitamin Smoothie

Ingredients

- 1/2 banana
- 1/2 tomato
- 1/4 cup papaya
- 1/2 cup spinach, chopped
- 1/4 green apple, chopped
- 1/2 cup Kale leaves, chopped
- Top with water

Directions

Fill half of the cup with the kale leaves. Add all the ingredients. Top up to the line with water. Blend thoroughly. Serve and enjoy.

Nutritional Information

- Calories 1
- Saturated Fat 0.2g
- Carbohydrate 31g
- Sodium 34mg
- Fiber 6g

Chapter 6 – 10 Smoothie Recipes for Radiant Skin

Are you trying to make your skin healthy?

Have all of your efforts been in vain?

If the answer to any of the aforementioned questions is yes, then try out these delicious smoothie recipes, and feel the difference to your ski.

Smoothie for Glowing Skin

Ingredients

- 1/2 cup avocado
- 1 cup coconut water
- 1 cup of Kale
- 1/2 apple
- 1 cup ice

Directions

Fill half of the cup with the kale. Add all of ingredients except the ice cubes. Top up with coconut water. Blend thoroughly. Serve with the ice cubes.

Nutritional Information

- Calories 242
- Saturated Fat 2.1g
- Carbohydrate 31g
- Sodium 288mg
- Fiber 12g

Pretty Pear Smoothie

Ingredients

- A handful of spinach and kale leaves
- 1/2 Asian pear, chopped
- 1/4 banana, frozen
- 1 tsp chia seeds
- 1/2 inch piece of ginger, freshly grated
- 1/4 tsp cinnamon
- 1 tsp flax seeds, grinded
- Top up with unsweetened Vanilla Hemp milk

Directions

Fill half of the cup with a mixture of spinach and kale leaves. Add all the ingredients. Blend thoroughly. Serve and enjoy.

Nutritional Information

- Calories 202
- Saturated Fat 0.7g
- Carbohydrate 30g
- Sodium 51mg
- Fiber 6g

Berry Medley Smoothie

Ingredients

- 1 cup spinach leaves
- 3/4 cup mixed berries, frozen
- 1/4 avocado
- 1 tsp ground flaxseeds
- 1 tsp unsweetened coconut flakes
- 1 tsp chia seeds
- Top up with almond milk

Directions

Fill half of the blender cup with the spinach leaves. Add the rest of the ingredients. Blend until smooth. Serve in a glass and enjoy the smoothie.

Nutritional Information

- Calories 200
- Saturated Fat 1.8g
- Carbohydrate 24g
- Sodium 209mg
- Fiber 9g

Green beauty Smoothie

Ingredients

- 1 cup coconut water
- 1/2 avocado
- 2 broccoli florets
- 1/4 cup apples, frozen
- 1 handful of spinach or Kale leaves
- a few pieces of diced cucumber
- Fresh ginger, grated

Directions

Fill half of the cup with a mixture of spinach and kale leaves. Add the rest of the ingredients to the cup. Top up with coconut water. Blend and serve. Optionally add 2-3 mint leaves.

Nutritional Information

- Calories 211
- Saturated Fat 2.1g
- Carbohydrate 26g
- Sodium 288mg
- Fiber 11g

Smoothie for Radiant Skin

Ingredients

- 1/4 banana, frozen
- 1 cup spinach and kale leaves combined
- 1/2 avocado
- 1 cup raspberries, frozen
- 2 tbsp cocoa powder, raw
- Top up with coconut water

Directions

Fill half of the blender cup with the spinach and kale leaves. Add the rest of the ingredients. Top up with coconut water. Blend thoroughly. Enjoy this drink and have radiant skin.

Nutritional Information

- Calories 348
- Saturated Fat 3.0g
- Carbohydrate 59g
- Sodium 293mg
- Fiber 17g

Wrinkle Fighting Smoothie

Ingredients

- 1/4 lemon juice and zest
- 1 cup low fat chocolate milk
- 1.5 cups berries, raspberries and strawberries, blueberries and blackberries in equal quantities
- A handful of Romaine and iceberg lettuce
- Top up with sweetened green tea
- A few ice cubes

Directions

Fill half the Nutribullet cup with the mixture of lettuce. Add the berry mixture. Top up with green tea. Blend thoroughly, serve with a slice of lemon & ice cubes.

Nutritional Information

- Calories 324
- Saturated Fat 0.5g
- Carbohydrate 75g
- Sodium 120mg
- Fiber 7g

Almond Flax Smoothie

Ingredients

- 1 tbsp flaxseed oil
- 1 small banana
- A handful of spinach leaves
- 1/2 cup organic apple juice
- 2 tbsp raw almond butter
- Ice cubes to add after blending
- 1/2 cup almond milk

Directions

Fill half of the Nutribullet cup with the spinach leaves. Add the rest of the ingredients with the exception of almond milk. Top up with almond milk. Blend thoroughly. Serve and enjoy this delicious filling smoothie.

Nutritional Information

- Calories 482
- Saturated Fat 2.8g
- Carbohydrate 45g
- Sodium 122mg
- Fiber 7g

Green Beautifier Smoothie

Ingredients

- 1 cup arugula
- 1/4 cup mango, chopped
- 1/4 cucumber
- 1/2 banana
- 1 tsp spirulina
- Coconut water

Directions

Fill half of the Nutribullet cup with the arugula. Add the rest of the ingredients. Top up with coconut water. Blend until smooth. Serve and enjoy.

Nutritional Information

- Calories 224
- Saturated Fat 0.8g
- Carbohydrate 52g
- Sodium 286mg
- Fiber 8g

Beautifying Smoothie

Ingredients

- 1/2 cup blueberries, frozen or fresh
- 1/2 orange, segmented
- 1/4 banana, ripe
- A handful of spinach leaves
- 1/4 cup strawberries, frozen or fresh
- 2 tbsp Chia seeds
- Coconut water

Directions

Fill half of the Nutribullet cup with the spinach leaves. Add the rest of the ingredients. Top up with coconut water. Blend thoroughly. Serve and enjoy.

Nutritional Information

- Calories 304
- Saturated Fat 1.2g
- Carbohydrate 56g
- Sodium 271mg
- Fiber 18g

Almond Milk Smoothie

Ingredients

- 1 cup almond milk
- 5 almonds, chopped
- 1/2 banana, chopped
- 1 cup kale, heaped, chopped
- 1/4 cup oats
- 5 apricots, chopped

Directions

Fill half of the Nutribullet cup with the kale leaves. Add the rest of the ingredients with the exception of almond milk. Top up with almond milk. Blend well. Serve and enjoy.

Nutritional Information

- Calories 400
- Saturated Fat 1.2g
- Carbohydrate 71g
- Sodium 213mg
- Fiber 14g

Chapter 7 – 10 Smoothie Recipes for Energy Boost

Smoothies are a great source of energy. They provide your body with such ingredients that help you in remaining active the whole day. When you start your day with one of the following smoothie recipes, you will be sure to have an energetic and wonderful day.

Killer Kale Smoothie

Ingredients

- 1 tbsp rice bran
- 1 banana, frozen
- 1 cup of kale, chopped
- 1 tbsp almond butter
- 1 tbsp Hemp seeds
- 1 cup almond milk

Directions

Fill half of the Nutribullet cup with the kale leaves. Add the rest of the ingredients. Top up with almond milk. Blend, serve and enjoy the smoothie.

Nutritional Information

- Calories 300
- Saturated Fat 1.6g
- Carbohydrate 44g
- Sodium 216mg
- Fiber 11g

Silky Blueberry and Chia Smoothie

Ingredients

- 1 cup coconut milk
- 1 tbsp honey
- A handful of spinach leaves
- 2 tbsp chia seeds
- 1 cup blueberries, frozen
- 1/2 cup softened, silk tofu
- 1 scoop of vanilla whey protein powder

Directions

Fill half of the Nutribullet cup with the spinach leaves. Add the rest of the ingredients. Top up with coconut milk. Blend well. Serve and enjoy this filling smoothie.

Nutritional Information

- Calories 956
- Saturated Fat 50.9g
- Carbohydrate 68g
- Sodium 209mg
- Fiber 18g

Shamrock Smoothie

Ingredients

- 1/4 tsp vanilla extract, pure
- 1/4 cup mint leaves, fresh
- 1/8 tsp mint extract, pure
- 1/2 apple, cored and diced
- 1 packet stevia
- 1/4 cup coconut milk, light
- A pinch of salt
- 1 cup organic baby spinach
- 1/2 banana, ripe

Directions

Fill half of the Nutribullet cup with the spinach leaves. Add the remaining ingredients to the cup. Blend thoroughly. Serve with ice cubes.

Nutritional Information

- Calories 139
- Saturated Fat 1.5g
- Carbohydrate 32g
- Sodium 38mg
- Fiber 6g

Beetroot and Apple Smoothie

Ingredients

- 1/2 gala apple, with core removed
- 1/4 cup coconut milk
- A handful of spinach leaves
- 1/2 cup chopped beetroot
- 1/4 inch piece of ginger
- The Juice of 1 lime
- 1/4 cup mixed berries, frozen
- 3 ice cube shavings
- Top up with coconut water

Directions

Fill half of the Nutribullet cup with the spinach leaves. Add the rest of the ingredients to the cup. Top up with coconut water. Blend thoroughly, serve and enjoy this smoothie.

Nutritional Information

- Calories 300
- Saturated Fat 12.9g
- Carbohydrate 42g
- Sodium 354mg
- Fiber 10g

Apple Pie Smoothie

Ingredients

- 1/2 apples cored and peeled
- 1/4 cup of cashew nuts, heaped
- Ice cubes shavings, as required
- 1 tbsp hemp protein
- 2 dates, pitted
- 1/2 cup of Romaine lettuce
- 1/2 banana, frozen
- 1 cup almond milk
- 1/2 tsp apple pie spice

Directions

Fill half of the Nutribullet cup with Romaine lettuce. Add the remaining ingredients. Top up with almond milk. Blend thoroughly. Serve and enjoy.

Nutritional Information

- Calories 502
- Saturated Fat 3.6g
- Carbohydrate 81g
- Sodium 197mg
- Fiber 13g

Spinach Peanut Butter Smoothie

Ingredients

- 1 banana, frozen and chopped
- 1 tbsp peanut butter, natural
- 1/2 cup Greek Yogurt
- 1 cup spinach leaves, fresh
- Top up with water

Directions

Fill half of the Nutribullet cup with the spinach leaves. Add the rest of the ingredients to the cup. Top up with water. Blend thoroughly. Enjoy this smoothie.

Nutritional Information

- Calories 282
- Saturated Fat 1.8g
- Carbohydrate 37g
- Sodium 152mg
- Fiber 5g

Cantaloupe and Lemon Smoothie

Ingredients

- Handful of Romaine lettuce
- 1/2 cup cubed cantaloupe
- 1/4 cup basil, fresh
- Zest of 1 lemon and the juice
- 1/2 cup watermelon, chopped
- Top with chilled water
- 2-3 ice cubes

Directions

Fill half of the Nutribullet cup with Romaine lettuce. Add the rest of the ingredients to the cup. Top up with water. Blend thoroughly. Enjoy this delightful smoothie with ice cubes and garnish with a sprig of mint leaves.

Nutritional Information

- Calories 73
- Saturated Fat 0.1g
- Carbohydrate 19g
- Sodium 34mg
- Fiber 3g

Sharon Fruit and Blackberry Smoothie

Ingredients

- 1 sharon/persimmon fruit, pitted
- 1 cup unsweetened coconut milk
- 1/2 banana, peeled and chopped
- 1/2 cup blackberries
- 1/2 cup baby spinach and baby kale (where available)

Directions

Fill half of the Nutribullet cup with the mixture of baby spinach and baby kale. Add the rest of the ingredients to the cup. Top up with coconut milk. Blend thoroughly and enjoy this delicious smoothie.

Nutritional Information

- Calories 662
- Saturated Fat 49.8g
- Carbohydrate 43g
- Sodium 49mg
- Fiber 11g

Dark Chocolate and Spinach Smoothie

Ingredients

- 1 cup raw spinach
- 1 scoop of protein powder
- 2 tbsp dark cocoa powder
- 1 cup blueberries, frozen
- 3 oz almond milk, unsweetened

Directions

Fill half of the Nutribullet cup with the spinach. Add the rest of the ingredients to the cup. Top up with almond milk. Blend and enjoy this heart healthy smoothie.

Nutritional Information

- Calories 228
- Saturated Fat 1.1g
- Carbohydrate 34g
- Sodium 236mg
- Fiber 9g

Blueberry Smoothie

Ingredients

- Fill half the cup with spinach
- 1 cup blueberries, frozen or fresh
- 1/2 cup chilled Green tea
- 1 tbsp Chia seeds
- 1/2 tbsp flaxseed oil
- Top with cold water

Directions

Fill half of the Nutribullet cup with the spinach. Add the rest of the ingredients. Top up with cold water. Blend thoroughly. Serve and enjoy this eyesight preserving smoothie.

Nutritional Information

- Calories 203
- Saturated Fat 1.0g
- Carbohydrate 28g
- Sodium 52mg
- Fiber 8g

Chapter 8 – 10 Smoothie Recipes for Anti-Aging

Protect your radiant beauty and youth trough these anti-aging smoothie recipes. Enjoy and have fun.

Antioxidant Anti-Aging Smoothie

Ingredients

- Fill half the cup with Romaine lettuce
- 1 cup beetroot (washed, peeled and diced)
- 1 whole lemon zest and juice
- 1/4 cup of cucumber
- Top up with coconut water

Directions

Fill half of the Nutribullet cup with the Romaine lettuce. Add the rest of the ingredients. Top up with coconut water. Blend, serve and enjoy this antioxidant rich anti-aging smoothie.

Nutritional Information

- Calories 106
- Saturated Fat 0.5g
- Carbohydrate 23g
- Sodium 615mg
- Fiber 9g

Beauty Bonanza Smoothie

Ingredients

- 1/4 cup strawberries, fresh or frozen
- A handful of kale leaves
- 1/2 cup blueberries, fresh or frozen
- 1/4 cucumber
- 1/4 tbsp chia seeds
- 1/4 cup silken tofu
- Top up with water

Directions

Fill half of the Nutribullet cup with the kale leaves. Add the rest of the ingredients. Top up with water. Blend well. Enjoy this beautiful drink with your friends.

Nutritional Information

- Calories 147
- Saturated Fat 0.4g
- Carbohydrate 26g
- Sodium 36mg
- Fiber 6g

Green Smoothie for Anti-Aging

Ingredients

- 1/2 cup spinach and kale leaves, heaped and chopped
- 5 grapes, green
- 1/2 pear, washed thoroughly and cored, leave the skin on
- 1 tsp chia seeds
- Top with water, cold if preferred

Directions

Fill half of the Nutribullet cup with the mixture of spinach and kale leaves. Add the rest of the ingredients to the cup. Top up with water. Blend until smooth. Serve with a sprig of mint leaves. Enjoy this fresh tasting anti-aging smoothie!

Nutritional Information

- Calories 83
- Saturated Fat 0.1g
- Carbohydrate 19g
- Sodium 14mg
- Fiber 4g

Coconut Bliss Smoothie

Ingredients

- Handful of kale
- 1 tbsp shredded coconut, unsweetened (leave some for garnish)
- Few pieces of cucumber
- 1/2 banana, frozen
- 4 oz cold coconut milk, unsweetened

Directions

Fill half of the Nutribullet cup with kale leaves. Add the rest of the ingredients but reserve a bit of the coconut for garnish. Top up with coconut milk. Blend until smooth. Serve the smoothie with the coconut garnish and enjoy.

Nutritional Information

- Calories 179
- Saturated Fat 7.8g
- Carbohydrate 25g
- Sodium 36mg
- Fiber 5g

Berry Smoothie

Ingredients

- 1/2 banana
- 1 tbsp flaxseeds, ground
- 1/4 cup blackberries
- 1/4 cup raspberries
- 1/4 cup blueberries
- A handful of spinach leaves
- 1/2 cup almond milk

Directions

Fill half of the Nutribullet cup with the spinach leaves. Add the rest of the ingredients. Top up with almond milk. Blend thoroughly, serve and enjoy.

Nutritional Information

- Calories 171
- Saturated Fat 0.5g
- Carbohydrate 31g
- Sodium 117mg
- Fiber 9g

Delectable Goodness

Ingredients

- 1/2 cup Kale, chopped
- The juice of 1 lemon
- 1/4 apple, medium, cored
- 1/4 orange, peeled and segmented
- 1/2 stick of celery, chopped
- A handful of fresh parsley
- Top up with coconut water

Directions

Fill half of the Nutribullet cup with the kale leaves. Add the rest of the ingredients. Top up with coconut water. Blend thoroughly, serve with a sprig of parsley and enjoy.

Nutritional Information

- Calories 117
- Saturated Fat 0.5g
- Carbohydrate 26g
- Sodium 307mg
- Fiber 7g

Chia and Blueberry Smoothie

Ingredients

- 1 cup of coconut water
- 1/2 cup of kale and spinach leaves
- 1 tsp coconut oil
- 1 tbsp chia seeds
- 1/4 cup banana, frozen
- 1/4 cup blueberries, frozen
- Ice, as needed

Directions

Fill half of the Nutribullet cup with the mixture of kale and spinach leaves. Add the other ingredients. Top up with coconut water. Blend until smooth, serve with ice cubes and enjoy.

Nutritional Information

- Calories 214
- Saturated Fat 4.0g
- Carbohydrate 35g
- Sodium 270mg
- Fiber 10g

Soy Milk Smoothie

Ingredients

- 1 cup water
- 3-4 ice cube shavings
- 1/2 tbsp ginger, chopped
- 1/2 cup of kale leaves and iceberg lettuce
- 1 cup soy milk
- 1 cup strawberries
- 2 tbsp honey

Directions

Fill half of the Nutribullet cup with the mixture of kale and iceberg lettuce. Add the rest of the ingredients to the cup. Top up with water. Blend until smooth. Serve.

Nutritional Information

- Calories 304
- Saturated Fat 0.6g
- Carbohydrate 59g
- Sodium 123mg
- Fiber 6g

Celery and Spinach Smoothie

Ingredients

- 1/2 green apple
- 1/2 cucumber, peeled
- 1 cup water
- 2 stalks of celery
- A handful of spinach leaves
- Juice and zest of 1 lemon. Save a slice for garnish.

Directions

Fill half of the Nutribullet cup with the spinach leaves. Add the rest of the ingredients to the cup. Top up the cup with water. Blend thoroughly. Serve with a slice of lemon. Enjoy.

Nutritional Information

- Calories 102
- Saturated Fat 0.2g
- Carbohydrate 25g
- Sodium 126mg
- Fiber 6g

Dewy Skin Smoothie

Ingredients

- 1/4 cup of papaya, chopped
- 1/4 dragon fruit, chopped
- A handful of Kale leaves
- 1 tsp ginger, fresh and chopped
- 1/4 cup mango, chopped
- 2 mint leaves
- Ice cubes
- 1/2 cup coconut water

Directions

Fill half of the Nutribullet cup with the kale leaves. Add the rest of the ingredients to the cup. Top up with coconut water. Blend thoroughly. Serve with the mint leaves and ice cubes. Enjoy this refreshing drink which is good for the skin.

Nutritional Information

- Calories 120
- Saturated Fat 0.3g
- Carbohydrate 27g
- Sodium 181mg
- Fiber 6g

Chapter 9 – 10 Smoothie Recipes for Super Foods

You must have heard a lot about super foods, well here are a few recipes that make excellent use of super foods, and provide all the essential ingredients your body requires.

Blueberry and Cocoa Smoothie

Ingredients

- 1 cup almond milk, unsweetened
- 1/2 banana
- Ice cubes
- 1 tbsp raw dark cocoa powder
- Handful spinach leaves
- 1/2 cup frozen blueberries
- 1 tbsp chia seeds

Directions

Fill half of the Nutribullet cup with the spinach leaves. Add the rest of the ingredients to the cup. Top up with the almond milk. Blend thoroughly. Serve and enjoy.

Nutritional Information

- Calories 204
- Saturated Fat 1.2g
- Carbohydrate 34g
- Sodium 208mg
- Fiber 11g

Mint Chip Smoothie

Ingredients

- 1 cup spinach
- 1/4 cup cashew nuts
- 1/2 tbsp cocoa nibs
- 1/2 banana
- 1 tsp vanilla extract
- 1 cup rice milk
- 1/2 cup coconut water
- 2 tbsp mint leaves, fresh. Leave one or two for garnishing
- 1/2 tsp honey, raw and pure

Directions

Fill half of the Nutribullet cup with the spinach leaves. Add the rest of the ingredients to the cup. Top up with coconut water. Blend well. Serve garnished with the left over mint leaves.

Nutritional Information

- Calories 540
- Saturated Fat 5.9g
- Carbohydrate 89g
- Sodium 229mg
- Fiber 8 g

Pineapple and Kale Smoothie

Ingredients

- 1 cup Pineapple
- 1 cup coconut milk and coconut water
- 2 tbsp shredded coconut, unsweetened
- 1/2 banana, ripe and frozen
- 1 cup Kale

Directions

Fill half of the Nutribullet cup with the kale leaves. Add the rest of the ingredients. Top up with coconut milk and water. Blend well. Serve and enjoy this exotic smoothie.

Nutritional Information

- Calories 750
- Saturated Fat 52.8g
- Carbohydrate 58g
- Sodium 69mg
- Fiber 13g

Raw Mint Chocolate Smoothie

Ingredients

- 1 cup almond milk
- 1 tbsp cocoa nibs
- 2 tbsp mint leaves, fresh
- 1/2 cup bananas, frozen
- 1 cup spinach leaves
- 1/2 vanilla bean, scraped
- A healthy pinch of salt

Directions

Fill half of the Nutribullet cup with the spinach leaves. Add the non-liquid ingredients to the cup. Top up with the almond milk. Blend thoroughly. Enjoy the minty chocolate smoothie.

Nutritional Information

- Calories 214
- Saturated Fat 6.9g
- Carbohydrate 35g
- Sodium 361mg
- Fiber 7g

Super Smoothie

Ingredients

- 1 cup baby spinach
- 1/2 inch of ginger, fresh and chopped
- 1 cup green tea, chilled
- 1/2 banana, frozen and chopped
- 1/2 cup pomegranate juice
- 1 cup ice cubes

Directions

Fill half of the Nutribullet cup with the baby spinach. Add the rest of the non-liquid ingredients. Top up with the pomegranate juice. Blend thoroughly. Serve with the ice cubes and enjoy.

Nutritional Information

- Calories 151
- Saturated Fat 0.2g
- Carbohydrate 36g
- Sodium 41mg
- Fiber 3g

Protein Smoothie

Ingredients

- 1 cup almond milk
- 1 cup spinach and kale leaves
- 1/4 cup almonds, raw
- 1 tsp coconut shreds, unsweetened
- 1/4 cup goji berries
- 1/2 banana, frozen
- 1 tbsp protein powder
- 1 tsp raw Brazil nuts, chopped

Directions

Fill half of the Nutribullet cup with the mixture of spinach and kale leaves. Add the rest of the non-liquid ingredients. Top up with the almond milk. Blend thoroughly. Serve.

Nutritional Information

- Calories 477
- Saturated Fat 2.6g
- Carbohydrate 53g
- Sodium 349mg
- Fiber 13g

Aloe Vera Lemonade Smoothie

Ingredients

- 1/2 cup Romaine leaves
- 1/4 cup Aloe Vera juice
- 1 lemon, zest and segments
- A pinch of salt
- 1 lime, zest and segments
- 1 apple cubed
- 5 green grapes
- 5 ice cube shavings
- Sprig of mint leaves

Directions

Fill half of the Nutribullet cup with Romaine lettuce. Add the other ingredients. Top up to the line with Aloe Vera juice. Blend thoroughly. Serve with the sprig of mint leaves.

Nutritional Information

- Calories 138
- Saturated Fat 0.1g
- Carbohydrate 37g
- Sodium 53mg
- Fiber 7g

Bananarama Smoothie Recipe

Ingredients

- 1.5 cup almond milk
- 1 tbsp coconut oil
- 1/2 cup mango chunks, fresh
- 1 cup carrots
- 1/2 cup strawberries
- 1/2 tsp honey, raw and natural
- 1 banana, fresh or frozen
- 1 cup spinach
- 2 tbsp Greek Yogurt
- 1 tbsp chia seeds
- 1 tsp bee pollen

Directions

Fill half the Nutribullet cup with the spinach. Add all the ingredients in Nutribullet, top with the almond milk, blend until smooth. Enjoy!

Nutritional Information

- Calories 506
- Saturated Fat 12.0g
- Carbohydrate 73g
- Sodium 398mg
- Fiber 15g

T-Mac Smoothie

Ingredients

- 1 cup water
- 1/2 cup blueberries, frozen
- 1 tbsp macadamia nut oil
- 1 cup kale
- 1 tbsp chia seeds
- 1/2 cup dark cherries, frozen
- A pinch of salt

Directions

Fill half the Nutribullet cup with kale, add in all the ingredients in a blender, top up with water. Blend thoroughly, serve and enjoy!

Nutritional Information

- Calories 313
- Saturated Fat 11.4g
- Carbohydrate 41g
- Sodium 4mg
- Fiber 9g

Cilantro Smoothie

Ingredients

- 1 pink grapefruit, whole
- 1 cucumber, chopped
- The juice of 1 lime
- A pinch of salt
- 1 cup pineapple
- 1/2 tsp agave nectar
- 2-3 cilantro, chopped
- 1/2 tsp vanilla extract, pure
- A pinch of cinnamon
- Top with water

Directions

Mix all the ingredients in a blender, blend until well combined. Enjoy this interesting smoothie!

Nutritional Information

- Calories 229
- Saturated Fat 0.2
- Carbohydrate 56g
- Sodium 18mg
- Fiber 4g

Chapter 10 – Reaping the Benefits from Fulfilling Smoothies

Now that you have learned the various benefits that smoothies have for you, along with all the recipes that have been provided in the book, you can be sure to have a scrumptious treat waiting for you.

All that needs to be done now is for you to try out the recipes, adjust the ingredients if you wish. Now is the time to go in your kitchens, take out your Nutribullet, and whip up these delicious smoothies. They are packed full of nutrition, have numerous benefits, and are satisfying, so much so you wouldn't feel the temptation to have a fat and sugar laden snack before you next meal.

Stop thinking and start whizzing. Once you get a taste of these delicious and fulfilling smoothies, you will keep coming back for more. So what are you still waiting for? Start blasting!

Printed in Great Britain
by Amazon